I0815325

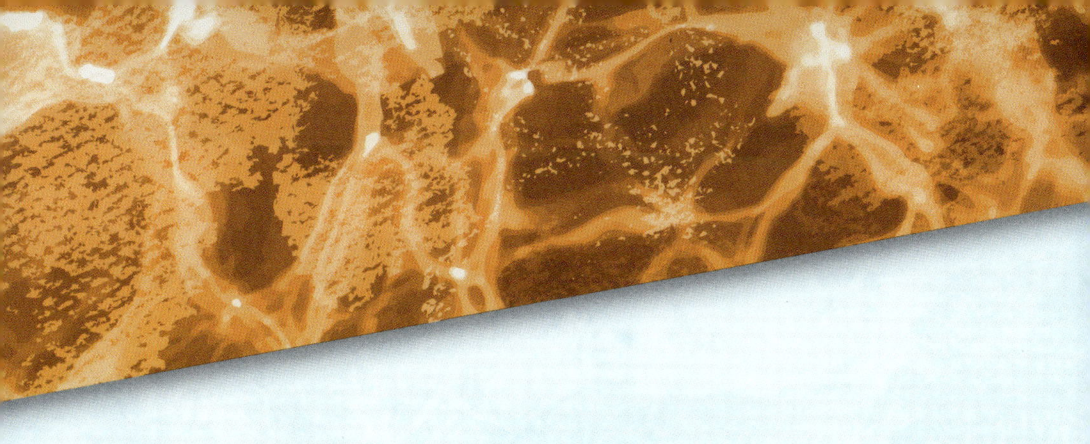

History of the Titanic

Cruise Ships Today

by Julie Murray

Dash!
LEVELED READERS
An Imprint of Abdo Zoom • abdobooks.com

Level 1 – Beginning
Short and simple sentences with familiar words or patterns for children who are beginning to understand how letters and sounds go together.

Level 2 – Emerging
Longer words and sentences with more complex language patterns for readers who are practicing common words and letter sounds.

Level 3 – Transitional
More developed language and vocabulary for readers who are becoming more independent.

abdobooks.com

Published by Abdo Zoom, a division of ABDO, PO Box 398166, Minneapolis, Minnesota 55439.

Printed in the United States of America, North Mankato, Minnesota.
102024
012025

Photo Credits: Alamy, Getty Images, Shutterstock
Production Contributors: Kenny Abdo, Jennie Forsberg, Grace Hansen, John Hansen
Design Contributors: Candice Keimig, Neil Klinepier

Library of Congress Control Number: 2024936556

Publisher's Cataloging in Publication Data

Names: Murray, Julie, author.
Title: Cruise ships today / by Julie Murray
Description: Minneapolis, Minnesota : Abdo Zoom, 2025 | Series: History of the Titanic | Includes online resources and index.
Identifiers: ISBN 9781098287238 (lib. bdg.) | ISBN 9781098287931 (ebook) | ISBN 9781098288280 (Read-to-me ebook)
Subjects: LCSH: Cruise ships--Juvenile literature. | Cruise liners--Juvenile literature. | Ocean travel--Juvenile literature. | Historic ships--Juvenile literature. | Titanic (Steamship)--Juvenile literature.
Classification: DDC 910.9163--dc23

Table of Contents

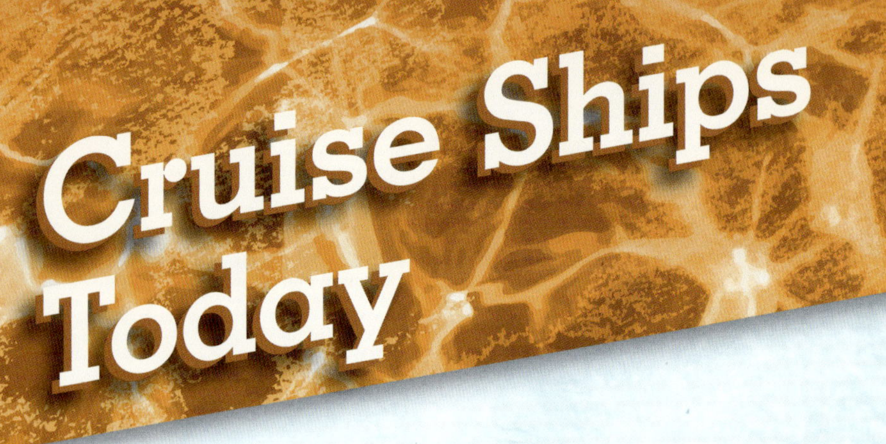

Cruise Ships Today

The **RMS** *Titanic* was a **luxury** ship that was built in 1912. Cruise ships today are even more impressive!

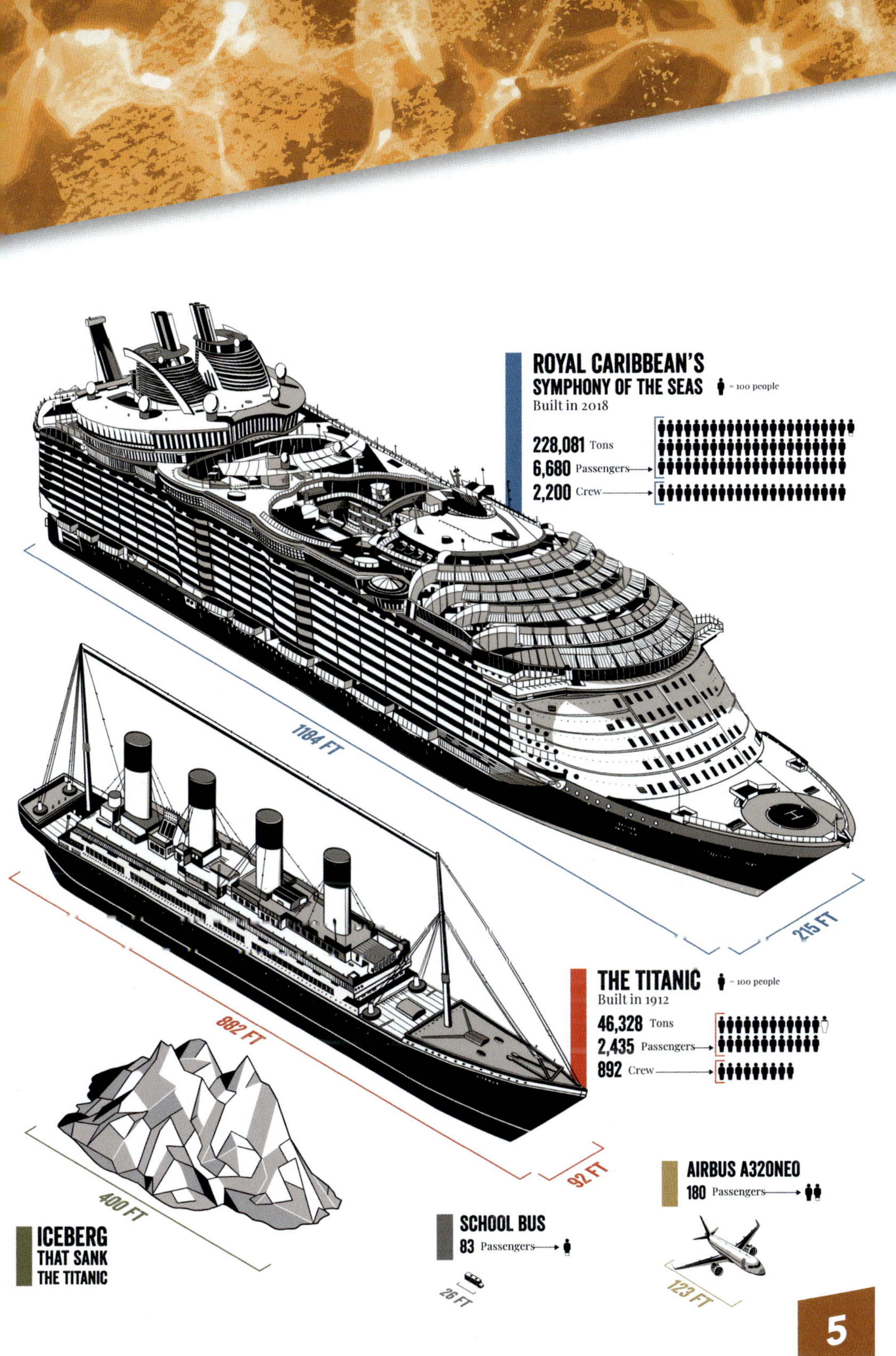
ROYAL CARIBBEAN'S
SYMPHONY OF THE SEAS
= 100 people
Built in 2018
228,081 Tons
6,680 Passengers
2,200 Crew
1184 FT
215 FT
THE TITANIC
= 100 people
Built in 1912
46,328 Tons
2,435 Passengers
892 Crew
882 FT
92 FT
400 FT
ICEBERG
THAT SANK
THE TITANIC
SCHOOL BUS
83 Passengers
26 FT
AIRBUS A320NEO
180 Passengers
123 FT

Today's cruise ships are like floating cities. The largest ship is 20 decks high and more than 1,100 feet (335 m) long!

There are plenty of things to do on cruise ships. From movie theaters to waterparks, there is a lot of fun to be had!

Cruise ships also have many restaurants. They have everything from buffets to **fine dining**. Coffee shops and ice cream parlors are on board too!

Safety at Sea

After the *Titanic* sank, many new laws were passed. These laws were made to improve safety at sea.

The Radio Act of 1912 requires ships to have **radio operators** on duty at all times.

HDG 138.5°
STW 0.1 kn
COG 170.5°
SOG 0.0 kn
ECDIS
Radar
Conning
Targets
Acquisition
AIS
Guard Zones
Guard Zone 1
Guard Zone 2
Enable "Lost tgt" warning
Range:
Activate AIS targets
RNG
CPA
TCPA
AIS
No ENC available
Review
Latitude
60°10.657' N
Longitude
025°13.507' E
Bearing
true
relative
153.8
015.3
Opp. Bearing
333.8
164.7
Range
2.47
NM
4575
Press Tab to edit manually

The International Ice Patrol formed in 1914. This organization **monitors** icebergs and their locations.

Ships also have lifeboat requirements. There must be enough lifeboats onboard for all passengers.

8
6
10

These laws are meant to keep cruise ships safe and save lives in the event of another disaster.

More Facts

- Each cruise ship has 1,000 to 2,000 crew members onboard.
- Royal Caribbean International's *Icon of the Seas* set sail in 2024. It holds an incredible 7,600 passengers!
- There were nearly 32 million cruise ship passengers in 2023.

Glossary

fine dining - a restaurant experience that is more sophisticated, unique, and expensive than at a typical restaurant.

luxury - something very pleasant but not necessary.

monitor - to observe in order to check on.

radio operator - someone who operates a radio transmitter or controls a radio system.

RMS - short for Royal Mail Ship.

Index

Online Resources

To learn more about cruise ships today, please visit **abdobooklinks.com** or scan this QR code. These links are routinely monitored and updated to provide the most current information available.